T0120712

THE POWER IN YOU

BRENDA ZYLSTRA

WESTBOW
PRESS®
A DIVISION OF THOMAS NELSON
& ZONDERVAN

Copyright © 2022 Brenda Zylstra.

All rights reserved. No part of this book may be used or reproduced by
any means, graphic, electronic, or mechanical, including photocopying,
recording, taping or by any information storage retrieval system
without the written permission of the author except in the case of
brief quotations embodied in critical articles and reviews.

This book is a work of non-fiction. Unless otherwise noted, the author
and the publisher make no explicit guarantees as to the accuracy of
the information contained in this book and in some cases, names
of people and places have been altered to protect their privacy.

WestBow Press books may be ordered through booksellers or by contacting:

WestBow Press
A Division of Thomas Nelson & Zondervan
1663 Liberty Drive
Bloomington, IN 47403
www.westbowpress.com
844-714-3454

Because of the dynamic nature of the Internet, any web addresses or
links contained in this book may have changed since publication and
may no longer be valid. The views expressed in this work are solely those
of the author and do not necessarily reflect the views of the publisher,
and the publisher hereby disclaims any responsibility for them.

Any people depicted in stock imagery provided by Getty Images are models,
and such images are being used for illustrative purposes only.
Certain stock imagery © Getty Images.

All Scripture quotations are taken from the King James Version.

ISBN: 978-1-6642-6654-4 (sc)
ISBN: 978-1-6642-6653-7 (e)

Print information available on the last page.

WestBow Press rev. date: 05/09/2022

CONTENTS

ONE

Who am I?

Haven't we all asked ourselves this question from time to time? Well believe me I really started asking myself this question when God said to me, "Write a book to help my sheep." More specifically He said, "Feed my sheep." I guess I have known for a long time about who I am. I am a person that ran hard from God. I ran from the truth. I ran from Beauty. I ran from love. I ran from acceptance. I ran from Grace. Running, running and running. I believed the lies that I was somehow unlovable, unchangeable, unreachable, and unforgivable. These are lies many of us believe. They are lies though.

Honestly, I have been pretty much everywhere on the spectrum. I have been so lost I never thought I would find myself or anyone else. I've been so alone in depression or grief that I honestly could not see anyone else or myself clearly. I have had moments of brilliance where I was on top of everything and I felt I didn't need anyone, or I thought I didn't need anyone. I have been so strong I felt invincible and so weak I wondered if I was having a stroke.

Truly I am no one. I am everyone. I am very much like you and nothing like you at the same time. You will find similarities and differences. I believe our similarities give us common ground, but our differences give us new perspectives, viewpoints, and incredible beauty in this world.

Our sameness helps us relate. Our differences help us grow and shape us. Our flaws give us beauty. Everything about us was perfectly designed by God for an exact moment in time. Every creature with a purpose. Every word spoken in its moment.

How wonderfully AWESOME does that make you and me? Just ponder for a moment about your life. Somewhere in your life you have said the exact perfect thing to someone. It has changed the course of their life. You taught someone something, helped them in some way. Made a difference. Most of the time you didn't even realize it. I have had some glimpses of a few things. Let's begin with my salvation story.

Everything really began when I was 5 years old in 1969 in a small church in Brownsville, Oregon. I would attend Sunday school and church with my grandparents on some Sundays. I made the choice to get saved one Sunday. Some people would argue that a child of that age can't really make that decision. God chooses you. You don't choose Him. You choose Him back. Your decision to follow him is a very important decision. I would encourage you to make that decision if you haven't. It is a life changer.

I grew up I was a normal kid. I had my rebellions. I did not really walk a Christian life. I would say a large percentage of my life I was very worldly. Smoking cigarettes and trying not to get caught by my parents, drinking with my friends at the movies and chewing gum so mom wouldn't know when I got home. I was a "normal" kid. Normal doesn't really exist but we all pretend there is something called normal. I followed the crowd. I tried to "be in charge" of my life most of the time and I made a great mess of it. One thing is for sure though, God was very much there. He did protect me. He did wait for me to wise up and say I need you God.

I did a lot of stupid things partying, experimenting with recreational drugs. (Marijuana and cocaine back in high school.)

People wanted to be around me for a little bit when I was happy, but they didn't really want to know me. I craved that more than anything. Yes, I have been vulnerable and made mistakes.

So why am I writing a book? I was told to. I will get to that later, but the real cincher came having coffee with a new friend. It was then that I realized that other people just like me have a hunger to be well. So many have the same struggles that I did. I can share what I know works with others and if I help even one person it's worth it.

You are worth it. You are unique. I never once gave thought to whether drugs could kill me, whether it was safe or anything like that. Everyone was doing it. (Not everyone was doing it). Seriously 1 marijuana joint is worth 5 cigarettes to your lungs as far as nicotine goes. Think about that. Cocaine destroys your heart valves. If you're making those choices, Think about it.

One time I got so high at a party I thought about taking my shirt off. There was a room full of high schoolers. I would have never lived that down. That was the last time I was not in control of myself. It is not safe for a young lady to be in a position like that. I question whether I was addicted to anything because of that. Also, I refused to go to work high. (My work performance was always a top priority to me. I would stop anything I was doing with ample wear off time to get to work and do a good job. Work ethic saved my life.) This in no way means I was making good or clear decisions. I was still in no way clear headed. After months of zero drugs, nicotine, and alcohol in my system I discovered quite by accident that my depression cleared up and I felt good. It takes months for your head to clear. Let that sink in.

I have known drinkers and marijuana users that get so high they can't function. If you do this and you do this often. You're out of control of your person. You are not being safe with yourself. The cold hard fact is in the world there are a multitude of quite horrible things that can happen to you in that state. If you are doing that, chances are someone is enabling you. How long do you think that person can take that behavior? Don't you think it scares them? Don't you think it would be nice for them to have a conversation with you that you remember? How many promises have you broken? I know you didn't mean to. How many times did they need you to be sober just that day or maintain just for a couple hours? I am not saying this to guilt you. I am saying this because it is true, and you need to wake up. Do it now before your liver is hurting and death is on its way. The cold hard truth is more people end up in the grave than getting help and off drugs and alcohol. Don't let it be you heading to the grave. You have no idea what an impact your life can make.

You never know what the impact of your words can have on someone. Everything is beautifully and wonderfully timed. You have an impact. You have no idea how important you are to this world. Maybe it is one small statement to one person at the perfect time. Maybe you will say that 200 times in your lifetime. Think of how many lives that impacts. Now if you can just ponder that 200 multiplied by the 200 lives, they may impact. What if my number is all wet and it is 1000 lives? What if it's more? How amazing is that? It could start with you.

One time I said something to someone that stopped them from using drugs. The statement I made was something I was thinking about myself at the time. It made the person think about their situation and they were empowered to stop using drugs at that point in their life. So many times, we do not know the impact of our words. There is something much deeper happening here. God's love. He loves us so much that He perfectly times encounters, words and ideas.

There is so much to the question, how wonderful am I? Recently I was overloaded at work. I talked to my project management coach later that day about this, her recommendation was simple but amazing and life changing. She said, "Ask your boss which item on your list she would like you not to do so you can accomplish that task, that way she can understand the impact various assignments have on your day." Talk about life altering. She changed my life in one phrase. I never thought of approaching my boss with a redirect of my duties.

How about you? Do you take on too much? Yes. It has always made me feel like I looked like a superhero to others. Guess what, it made me look like I have nothing better to do. I always wondered why this happened to me. I looked like I didn't have anything to do. Do you have what you need to manage time so that your 20% is so effective that the other 80% just needs to be the diligence stuff? (Your calls, filing, material gathering, and coordinating.) Make your important part be the important part.

Let's go deeper. Perceptions other people have of us are not what we think. I do not know the exact percentage, but I would venture to say most of the time you are wrong if it's negative. Say I'm in production I want the time of day when the boss walks by to be an active time. Even if my machine is broken, I want to be discussing where I can help with my manager or sweeping or something especially when important people walk by. I also want to take my breaks. You need to regroup. (If you overproduce and the next guy can't keep up, everything fails.) Steady progress. (It was super hard for me to learn.)

Now let's talk more about perceptions. Have you ever thought people don't like me? People think I'm ugly. People think I'm fat. People think I'm stupid. People think I'm too thin, white, purple, orange, or scruffy? Most of the time people are making grocery lists in their head. Dwelling on their own "stuff." MOST people are not even thinking of you at all. They are thinking about what's for dinner or what they said to their child or spouse. So, make friends with your skinny, or chunky body, or out of place hair. Our flaws are what make us unique and beautiful. There is a wonderful Ted Talk on Not Taking Things Personal. I highly recommend it. It will bring a new level of understanding to perceptions for you.

If you were to meet my husband, you might look at him differently than I do. To me, he is the most handsome man in the world. He is my Mr. Universe. He thinks I am the most beautiful woman in the world. (Please don't tell him that I am not Miss America he's happy.) Thank you, Lou, for being the love of my life. You're the best change I ever experienced. Thanks for always being the handsomest man ever and believing I'm the most beautiful woman in the world. Thank you for showing me I don't have to do it all and I don't have to do it by myself. Thank you for being on my team.

Your perceptions can even be stronger you may have an interaction at work that has you thinking you're going to get fired. Or maybe something happens between a coworker and you, and you are sure that they are out to get you know. Maybe you think someone is after your job. If this sounds like you, there is a chance you may have anxiety. I have some tips in this book on that. There will be more in a future book about that. There are many books out there on anxiety though I highly recommend getting one and learning some techniques to work through your thought patterns. Change what you are saying to yourself, and you change your whole life. God is always loving you. No matter how many mistakes you've made He sent His only begotten son just to have a relationship with you. He is always good, always in your corner, always loving you and wants you to know Him.

Finding love and beauty in yourself takes time. There are many methods. Meditating on this scripture can help. There are so many great scriptures I could make this book to heavy for you to carry if I went into the depth of God's love that is poured out in each page of the bible. I encourage you to explore this for yourself. I have included some examples in this book to begin your search.

Philippians 4:8 "Finally, brethren, whatsoever things are true, whatsoever things *are* honest, whatsoever things *are* just, whatsoever things *are* pure, whatsoever things *are* lovely, whatsoever things *are* of good report; if *there be* any virtue, and if *there be* any praise, think on these things."

Love comes when you are ready. Make yourself ready and don't search. Keep your eyes open but make sure you are doing the things you need to do to make a great life with someone. Preparing yourself to be the person you need to be, to be that loving significant other. Learn the scriptures based on love. Begin with God's love and opinion of you and you can't go wrong. When you accept Christ into your life you become whole. You have every feature of Christ within you. His peace, love, healing, longsuffering, joy, grace, and answered prayer are just a few gifts from the well of salvation.

You are a child of God. You were handpicked. Placed at this moment at this time. What could be more special than that?

You are lovely just the way you are. Someone will look at you like you are the most amazing person that has ever walked into their life. Wait for that.

The Truth shall set you free. How many times have you thought that person doesn't like me? Does it matter? Has your perception created a friction that made you treat them differently? If you had treated them with kindness and walked away more, would it have changed? I have watched this work in my own life. Begin to view yourself and others the way God sees you. When we look at each other through His eyes that changed perspective and lens of love will give you the grace to work with anyone. Even the most hurting individuals can be changed with love.

I worked in manufacturing and as an electrician's apprentice. I loved electrical work. I am also very hardheaded. I tried more than anyone to make manufacturing and the electrician field work for me. The brutal truth is I would never be more than mediocre at either one. I understood the principals, had the eye hand coordination but was such a perfectionist that I could never really be fast at it. It was not meant to be. Maybe in 30 years I would be good at it. Let's add some perspective to that statement. 30 years from now I will be in my late 80's and electrical work might be something I am not as interested in doing. Haha.

Something wonderful happened though. My health changed. My love for the electrical field would never have allowed me to stop. My strength failed me due to a few health issues. As I said before, I am stubborn, so it took a few bricks to the forehead for me to give in and realize I had to stop. Safety won, when I could not lift safely, I had to think of others that might be lifting with me when my off and on strength failed. Gratefully my health came back. Not all my strength came back yet. I'm still working on that. I don't like to give up. I did have to leave the electrical field for my safety and others.

I am not a person who looks at the closed door for very long. I learned this from my many devastating layoffs and a brilliant mom that never quit. The next job was always better. So, get excited if something horrible happens to you. Something better is coming. Look for it. Please don't waste time whining at that closed door. If you do only spend a day. It is not worth wasting the time on.

When I could not be an electrician anymore. I sat right down, looked at my skills and said, "What fits my skills? What CAN I do?" I had a lot of former administrative skills. I decided to take a project management course. 5 months later I had a job as a Safety and Quality coordinator in mattress manufacturing for a wonderful company and my administrative career was up and running. Two years later I was working closer to home as a technical writer and got my first project management opportunity. Don't be afraid to reinvent yourself. There is a terrific recruiter out there named Andrew Lecivita that has a ton of tips for you. Right there on You Tube.

It did not make me happy to have to let go of years of hard work to get somewhere in the electrical field. I would still love to be an electrician. No means no though. When you are physically unable to do something anymore and you must settle for being able to lift your arms above your head instead of lift things above your head. Make the right choice. There is still something you will love to do out there. It is just a change in direction.

Perceptions and people. You can change it with your attitude. I've turned enemies into friends. I've seen misunderstood people blossom at work with a little help and training. All it takes sometimes is a little interest and a little help. Some kindness. Just taking a moment to try to help a person understand can make a difference. If someone thinks everyone hates them, they are not going to do well in that environment. Remember, God loves everyone. You can too.

Let's talk polish for a minute. When I was 19, I received a piece of advice that has stuck with me and been most helpful, "Polish your attitude." (I'm so sorry Sergeant that I cannot remember your name to credit you.) My land navigation sergeant was wise. This piece of advice has served me well over the years. Thank you, sergeant, for a gem that got me through some tough spots.

Working with people can be a challenge. Over the years I've worked with great teachers, and a many polishers. I am grateful for both.

My early years were filled with people that just moved people on if they "weren't a good fit". I honestly don't know if it's management or HR that has grown from there. I do know that polish is a great thing. If you allow difficulty to polish you, there are no limits to your growth potential. My current company has a saying "rock is hard, water is wet." Their meaning is things are as they are. Facts are facts. I believe water polishes and changes rock though in time. Polish your attitude always makes me smile and work on myself.

Sometimes just listening to someone is all it takes. One time I was very angry with a coworker about something they said. I listened to that person even though at first, I did not agree. After hearing what they really meant, I understood why they were saying what they were saying, and it completely made sense. When someone makes you angry. That is when you need to listen. Life is about polish.

We are all different for a reason. We are here to help each other. Individuals with their unique talents working together, collaborating to create something better than just the one person could create. Groups being better than the sum of their parts.

There is only 1 of you in the whole world. Just one. There is a specific thing that you are super good at. There is a moment in time that it will be perfectly timed for someone. A friend will need help with a resume, and you will have the right words. Someone will need help with their car, and you will know how to fix it or know the right mechanic. Everything perfectly timed. This is a great thing. If you do not understand someone, try to see things from their side. They have a different viewpoint. It will open a whole new perspective to you. Learning to understand them will open doors and windows for you that you can not imagine. Be open to it. That person is your polishing stone. Give a big woohoo.

I ask you to begin right now to believe the truth about yourself. You are a loved child of God with limitless capability. Then you can believe in others too. All of us can work together. Polishing each other.

TWO

How Did I Get Here?

I know. That's easy for you to say. Your life is going well. OK. It hasn't always been sunshine.

Life isn't always going to hand your roses and tell you you're wonderful. There are going to be days that are hard. Yes, I still have hard days. I catch colds and I get sweaty when I work in the hot sun. (I like working hard. My body doesn't allow as much now but I do what I can.) I have days that hurt so bad I don't want to get up, but I get up and work that out. I had many dark days before I got to where I am today.

When the time changes, I struggle with depression in the winter. The continuous darkness is hard for me to keep my spirits up. I must use every tool I've got to stay above water during the dark cycle of winter.

November and December also bring bad foods. Sweets and carbs no one needs. Pies, cookies, and parties, oh my. Sometimes people have unhealed emotions with family that make holidays difficult. Thankfully I've worked through that. I recommend you find a way to get back to the love with your family if possible. Many things can throw you off balance in a heartbeat.

Here is one you may not have thought of medical or dental work. Any type of trauma to the body or anesthesia can throw your body off a little. Drink lots of water and remember you might be a little off normal. Go to the dentist and doctor though. You need to keep yourself healthy. I am not saying stay away from health professionals. Do what you need to do to stay healthy.

There was a time in my life when things were very bleak and dark. Darkness almost consumed me. I suffered from depression for 36 years. I was on anti-depressants off an on. They would work for awhile then become ineffective. I planned my death 4 times but each time something got in the way of my accomplishment. I self-medicated with drugs and alcohol. Also, ineffective. I tried many things that were ineffective. I learned just prior to writing this book that it may have been anxiety all along and negative thought patterns not depression. The tools still worked though, and I am grateful.

Do you suffer with depression? If you do, you are not alone. Very few people speak out but there are so many out there struggling is silence and darkness. If you are thinking about suicide right now, please think about this. Suicide shares your pain. It spreads it to someone else. It destroys more than your life. It makes those around you wonder what they could have done to help you. It hurts those close to you making them wonder why you didn't talk to them. It causes family arguments about what people could have done and blame circles and cycles. So please talk to someone. Get help. Stop drugs and alcohol. The temporary fix they provide makes you worse off.

I agonized over whether to tell this part of my story because I am not who I once was. It is unpleasant to remember who I was, and it is embarrassing to admit that you were once very lost. Sometimes we must face our demons. If it helps one person, it's worth it.

During my teenage years I began to want to fit in. Well, fitting in is hard because you weren't designed to "fit in". You were designed to be "outstanding". Like most teenagers fitting in was the most important thing to me. Every one of us is made special, individually crafted, unique. We are designed for community but we are unique so we can share our gifts with each other and help each other. If we were all the same, we could not accomplish much. Our uniqueness allows us the ability to grow and help each other in truly amazing ways. My uniqueness always made me feel like I was from another planet. Like I never belonged anywhere including my own family.

Fitting in as a teenager was easier if you did something unacceptable. Sharing a secret makes you part of an "in" crowd. Smoking, drinking, or doing drugs were the "in" things of my time sadly and unfortunately, I was not smart enough to see the trap. The lie. The fact of the matter was I was a 4.0 student that did not want to be called brain. I had great Christian friends that were very nice, and I did not have to do anything to be their friends. I had friends from junior high that were and are amazing and I didn't have to be anything but me. Instead, I started smoking to be "cool." I look back now and think I looked like a monkey face. Ha ha. Once you're doing that, what is one more thing.

I experimented a little with drugs in high school. A little alcohol, cigarettes, and marijuana. Here and there. Then I joined the military and only continued smoking. Probably not the best choice. Running and smoking don't really make great partners. The military was great for me except the drinking age was lower in some states and loneliness was something I always felt no matter where I was.

If you often feel alone and like you don't fit in. I would like to reassure you that it is perfectly normal. We all fit in, but we all don't fit in. We are all the same, but we are all different. Our similarities give us something to talk about. Our differences give us something we can help each other grow with. We were never meant to be the same. That is so we can help each other. Like I said before, the inventor needs help with inventory, or typing, or maybe bookkeeping. The mechanic needs someone to answer phones. You don't want to interrupt your train of thought while troubleshooting a mechanical or electrical problem. We are different so we can help each other. It is ok that you are different. Celebrate it.

Back to the story, my drinking got heavier and heavier. The drinking made me do stupid things. Now you can't blame everything on alcohol. I was never a black out drunk. I always remembered what I did and spoke. Mostly because I never felt safe around anyone. I never trusted anyone enough to just let go. I had to always keep my wits about me. No matter what drug or alcohol I tried, I felt I needed to be able to have presence of mind to get away if I needed to. I did not trust anyone. I did have a few times that were out of control but mostly I stuck to this. I had to make sure I could keep my physical person safe. Women must always protect themselves from people who seek to take advantage. Human trafficking has been around a long time. Not just in this millennium.

I worked hard to make sure I always had my own place to go to. The military training was very good at teaching me to make sure I always knew every exit and how to get away from anyone I was around. I wasn't afraid because I could handle any situation. I stayed in shape and alert.

Hand in hand with the drinking I searched for love. I searched for trust. I talked to people all the time. Only I had no idea how to go about it. I was strong and capable and came off too strong. This just ended up seeming promiscuous and that wasn't my intention but with the drinking the lines were blurred. My outgoing nature also sparked rumors of promiscuity that I had a hard time shaking. Appearances aren't always what they seem. You can't open your heart when you don't trust anyone. You can't love when you don't love yourself. I didn't really know who I was by this point.

After leaving the military for an electrical career, the drinking got worse. The lost feeling got worse. The drugs got worse. Eventually I began using meth on weekends. This would have been a complete disaster if I did not have a strong work ethic. I always had a job. Always had to be to work at a certain time and had to be sober to go to work. Probably saved my life. Even if you are an occasional meth user you are not in your right mind. Stop using 6 months and you will understand what I mean by that.

I decided to quit in 1995. Six months later I woke up one day and realized I felt good for a change. I wasn't depressed. I felt happy for a depressed person.

My drinking was still a problem but hey life wasn't so bad. Two years later I took a healing class. One of the requirements of the class was to give up alcohol for 2 weeks before the class.

Before that class, I was thinking one day, so what if I'm an alcoholic. I'm not hurting anyone but me. It isn't ok. Alcoholism eventually leads to black outs, not being able to remember conversations, memory loss, liver damage and eventually youthful death. People have died in their 20's from alcohol poisoning. Liver failure by the mid-fifties. Your family and friends don't want this for you.

I took the healing class. After the class I did not desire to drink like I did before. I made friends with me. I would go months or years without having any alcohol. It just didn't cross my mind anymore.

So there seemed to be a correlation with my friendship with who I was and what I was doing. Please make friends with that person in the mirror. You may think you are friends but if you are damaging your body, are you friends? Loving who you are means caring for yourself.

Making friends with the person in the mirror wasn't easy for me. My first life coach said, "Look yourself in the eye and tell yourself I love you." That took me several months to accomplish. It was worth doing. I recommend this even if you start with you have a nice nose or chin. Keep trying. Make friends with you.

Here is what I learned in Alanon. Addicts don't take care of themselves. Many of them can never be good enough. Addicts tend not to get dental work done, tend not to go to the doctor.... Are you putting that stuff off? Take care of yourself. These are generalities. If you are falling down from drinking or drugs does that sound like you are taking care of yourself? If you can't remember the conversation with your kid or spouse, are you taking care of your relationships?

If you are in that boat what will help you are 4 things. 4 are most important. I did these things, and they work. If you can work number 5 in, you will be much happier.

1. Exercise – There is a way. Unless you are bed ridden. You can move something. The body is made for motion. Take a couple steps. If you have heart or lung issues talk to your doctor about what you can safely do to work muscle.

2. Nutrition – Balance your nutrition. I eat 4 vegetables, 4 proteins, 2 fruits, 2 carbs, 1 seeds and nuts, 1 healthy fat, and 3 teaspoons. (Teaspoons are Oils, butter....) If you are not the same size as me Your nutritional requirements will be different. I don't want some 6-foot 200-pound man trying to eat like a 5-foot 160-pound woman. (That is not my ideal weight.) I am a work in progress and that is all anyone should ever ask of you.

3. Spirituality – You need to feed your spiritual self. Read your bible. Do a bible study. Take a class in your spiritual liking. (There are many religions. I am not going to tell you which one is right. Everyone thinks they are right. Find a comfortable doctrine to you. I think Jesus would have wanted us to know him and be comfortable with him).

4. Gratitude – Write 3 things down that you are grateful for. Do this in the morning and in the evening. Get a notebook and fill it up. Doesn't matter how it starts. My first entries were hard because I was depressed. I was grateful to make it through the day. Just start it gets better.

5. Learn something knew – This is a self esteem thing. No one can take something you know from you. Bettering yourself is something you do for YOU. It's all yours.

If you are an addict, there are many programs. You can contact your doctor and find out if you don't know whether you are an addict or not. You might just be suffering from depression and self-medicating to not deal with reality. Recovery now through churches, AA, Serenity Lane, and a multitude of inpatient and outpatient sources. Please get help. There are so many people that love you and are waiting for that. Building relationships isn't easy after addiction but you can do it. I have the love of an amazing man in my life. My life is so amazing without drugs and alcohol being the center. Eventually there will be one more. I have a lot of research and learning to do before I can fully help you though.

I believe mental health is the problem. No, I am not saying you have a mental health issue. It is my belief that most people suffering from alcoholism and drug addiction are really suffering from depression, anxiety, loneliness, trauma, or some sort of mental health issue. Solve that and that self-medicating will resolve itself.

I just found out about anxiety. Just realized that I have a little bit of it, a coworker has it, a couple of friends have it and someone I am close to is affected by it a lot. I am grateful my coworker shared something about it, or I would have been completely unaware. This changed my life. My information on this is limited so there will be in another book. What I do know is that using some of the techniques have really helped me to deal with my own anxiety and other people's anxiety in a manner that has reduced a lot of stress in my life and the life of others.

Let's get back to Darkness. You would think my darkness would have ended with my struggle with depression being over. I only had 2 pieces of the puzzle. I began exercising. I was learning new things. (I'm always doing that. I like learning.)

I came to a point in my life where I was struggling in my relationships. No one knew me because I worked all the time.

It was a low economy time, and I was in a low pay position with less than 40 hours a week and no health insurance when my appendix got a hole in it. Get your nutrition on track people. It's important. The surgery for that cost around $30,000. That was in 2011. Medical prices never go down just like education prices.

I mentioned before, I spent my whole adult life working. Sometimes 2 jobs or 1 job and night school. My family barely knew me. No one knew me. I never once tried getting close to people. Not since high school. I believed that letting anyone close to you would only result in them using any information they could get against you. Only 3 people in my life had never done that to me. I wasn't about to let people in.

After the surgery, I sat at home thinking how am I going to get out of this mess. Darkness consumed me. I contemplated ending my life again once again my life felt without purpose. What was the point in continuing? I truly had no way to pay for any of the things I needed to pay for. My marriage was in ruin. My family barely knew me. It all seemed so bleak. That was when I felt the most amazing light come over me. I knew it was Jesus. I said, "If you can make something of this mess that I have made of my life, it is yours."

God wasted no time. The next day my surgery bill went from $28,900 to $4,500. The payments were manageable for my budget too. Two weeks later I got a 2 dollar raise and a 40 hour a week job. 2 months later I got another $1.41 raise and got into an electrician's apprenticeship. I got regular raises after that until another seemingly bad thing happened. That worked into steady pay that evened my income out over the year and I lost nothing.

Anyway, I kept my focus on God. He has not steered me wrong. I learn each day about Him. That focus helps me not be thrown when life throws a curve. The more I learn about God, the more I know of His Goodness and love. He truly does love us.

Believe me people can change. The person I described doesn't reside inside me anymore. I did a lot of work to get here. It's all about small steps. I didn't change overnight. I still make mistakes and each new learning about God shows me more that I can change and do better. The bible is full of people that weren't perfect, but one thing is sure, God loved them. He loves you too.

Let's talk about the power of 20 minutes. I can't remember if I got this from Terri Saville Foy or James Clear. (Both excellent authors. I recommend their time management and declutter your life books.) Anyway, agree with yourself to set aside 20 minutes a day. Now sit down with your gratitude notebook and figure out what you are going to do with that 20 minute to change your life. It can be anything. Cleaning Monday, Declutter Tuesday, Walking Wednesday, Spending time with your child Thursday, Reading Friday…. Whatever you want. There are endless possibilities of what you can do with your life.

There is only 1 of you in the whole world. Just one. There is a specific thing that you are super good at. There is a moment in time that it will be perfectly timed for someone. A friend will need help with a resume, and you will have the right words. Someone will need help with their car, and you will know how to fix it or know the right mechanic. Everything perfectly timed.

Jesus is the most powerful tool you can have against depression, anxiety, or addiction. When you invite Jesus into your life something amazing happens. I am certain that you have heard that he comes into your life and cleanses your spirit. (Makes you whiter than snow). Do you know what that means?

THREE

· ·

Look Where You're Going
And walk away from addiction

The first step in life they say is the hardest. Who are they? Well pretty much all the experts. Statistically speaking inertia is not your friend. Inertia – A tendency to do nothing and remain unchanged. Guess what. Once again you are not alone. Many people fail to start. Take a walk with me as we unveil addictions and how to walk away from them. Let's walk away from addiction together.

I know of a few reasons people become addicted there are probably more, but these are the few I am aware of and I think so many people fall under. One type that I know personally are self-medicators that are trying to make their depression/anxiety/possibly other mental disorders go away by drinking or using drugs. Another type is not wanting to face the pain of some trauma in their life. Both types can walk away from addiction. There is hope but you will need to work on your inner self.

Are you an addict? Do you have a problem with drugs, alcohol, or something else? OK here is a look in the mirror for you if you are asking yourself that question. If you feel like you have to hide it from people, there is a good possibility you have a problem. If it is something that's frequency has taken over some of your hobbies and friendships, there is a good possibility that you have a problem. If it is interfering with your work or relationships, you have a problem. I am personally inviting you to walk away from that right now. Let God in your life and let him heal you from it. I can't promise you it will be easy, but I can promise you it will be worth it. Let Him in your life and He will do the rest. He has guided me every step. Let's look where we are going. Accept Jesus into your heart and He will cleanse you and set you free from your bondage. He will release you from craving.

I don't know that I can call myself an addict where drugs and alcohol are concerned but certainly to sadness, cigarettes, cheese, and sugar. There are many kinds of addiction. You do not have to be chained to anything. Set yourself free.

1 John 5:4 KJV Whosoever believeth that Jesus is the Christ is born of God: and this victory that overcometh the world, even our Faith.

This is what gives you the power to walk away right now. Jesus gave us the power to overcome everything in this world. It is more than that though. When you receive Christ, you receive the holy ghost inside you. That is power. You receive the power of Christ in you. You receive healing, answered prayer, freedom from the bondage of drugs and alcohol, freedom from sickness, and resurrection power just to mention a few of the gifts of salvation. If that doesn't get you excited, you're not paying attention. You are God's child. He loves you no matter what.

When I first was called to write this book, I was very focused on this chapter. I wondered how much should I talk about my past? Am I healed enough to go through it again? Would I be protective enough of those still in it? Addicts need love and support to get to their release.

The truth is I have watched friends become something they are not. Personalities completely change. People do things they would never do because they aren't in their right minds. I've seen myself become something I'm not. I've been that silly little party girl no one thought had feelings, that people easily discard and disregard. I have watched friends become so addicted they just go down the path to death. 10 percent of my books will be gifted to addicts in hopes that I can make a small difference. If I help one, it's worth it. I admit that I hope I help more.

Please stop if you are using drugs. Your family, no matter how wounded and hurt they are inside, loves you and wants you to live. They want you to become a whole person, a healed person. They want you to be alive not the empty shell you have become of yourself.

I have been the person that was confused by a drug rattled mind. It took 6 months for my head to clear enough to think straight. I woke up one day after 6 months and said to myself "hey I feel good." The end of my use was by accident. I broke contact with the people, and it just wasn't around. At first, I wanted to continue using. I was fortunate that it wasn't around. I had the blessing that I realized I felt better. My mind was so messed up I couldn't see it would have led to the same thing.

It is so important to take that first step. That first step puts you in the top 20 percent. Starting is all it takes to begin a new life. Then the real work begins. You can do this.

Support can help a great deal. You need a positive peer group to keep you going. Good friends, support groups, online chat rooms, or any form that fits your life. You can do this. I believe in you. Eventually I will start my own program to help the people that the 12-step program missed. I know there are people that don't want to go to those meetings and be reminded every week of what they did when they were high or drunk. Reliving it isn't always helpful. I believe it holds them in a stuck place. I want to create a program that moves the former addict forward. Give them life again. Show people they can reenter life without drugs and alcohol. Really live and be passionate about something.

The reason some succeed, and some don't is focus. Find something that keeps you motivated. Usually, a reason why. Keeping your focus centered on doing something is helped a great deal if you have a reason for doing it. Better health, wanting to be there for your kids or family, wanting to live a better life, or any reason that will hold you accountable. Get your why and hold onto it. When I quit smoking, I did it so I could breathe better. I wanted to go upstairs without being out of breath. I wanted to live a longer healthier life.

A great example is a diabetic sticking to their nutrition and exercise plan because they want to be healthy and be able to see well. Keep your motivations positive.

(Focus on what is lovely, what is true) You are not trying to bring unhealthy. You are not trying to bring bad things like blindness. Make sure your statements are positive. No Fear statements. Fear is a bad motivator. Fear will motivate you until you are out of danger. We want to stay motivated.

People can and can't be good motivators. Make sure it is a buddy that will stick with you and help motivate you. Not one that is going to say, "oh that's ok we know you're a failure." Don't pick a friend that expects you to fail. You know who they are. You want friends that believe in you. If you have been using drugs or alcohol you may struggle with support at first. You may need to just rely on yourself until you rebuild that trust. You can do this in time. I believe in you.

Motivators are so important, and you need more than one. Try to think of 3 to 5. If what you want is important you can come up with at least 3 why's. Write them down right now. Put it in the front of your gratitude journal.

Plan, Plan and Plan. You need to have a plan and at least a contingency plan or two. There are a couple of things I know about starting something knew. Something will shift. Especially if it's a great God given idea. The moment you begin that devil will throw everything at it.

When I started my book? No one knew about it. It was peaceful. I contacted a publisher. Suddenly my dad calls early in the morning before his fishing trip. My husband calls on his way to work. All kinds of interruptions in my normally peaceful alone writing time. Distraction after distraction came. Nope. Not letting it stop me. I continued to write.

Change my day, move my time, rearrange my schedule but I will continue my book. It will settle down. Back off Devil. God said do it and I intend to do it. I will not let any distraction get in my way. Now that is the kind of focus, I am talking about. Disciplined. I can dodge this, if I need to pivot and move in another direction to accomplish this downstream focus that is what I will do. That is where you are going too. Focus on that goal and don't let go.

I will work on my goal no matter what. That is what you will do. Get the kind of focus that refuses to be broken. You've got this.

Seriously people. It takes months to realize what you did to yourself. I love you. Please stop doing this. I do not care what you think you did to deserve it. You don't deserve that. You may think you are just having fun, real fun is being fully engaged in doing things you really enjoy doing. Building something, creating something, fishing, working on a project, spending time with your kids, or helping someone are all things that will make you feel better than any drug or alcohol. Go hiking, site seeing, paint, talk with a friend, see a relative you've wanted to see or try a new hobby. Even if it is slow at first it will be more rewarding than drugs or alcohol if you give it some time.

Begin your healing journey. It is once again the same as the depression cycle. Gratitude and exercise. You must look at the world the way God wants you to. Look up. God loves you,

you can too. God is always looking out for us. You just need to focus on what is lovely, what is true. Get a bible. Start with the New Testament. You can get to the Old Testament later when you want to. I'm pretty sure God doesn't care where you start. He just wants you to start. He loves us and will guide our mistakes and make them beautiful. Just as He made each one of us beautiful. We are not a mistake though.

He wants to guide every moment of your day. He loves you even more than I do. He loved you first, before you were born.

Now gratitude helps. So, every morning when you get up write down the first thing you are grateful for. Same thing when you go to bed. Try to think of 3 things. Get a cheap dollar store notebook and fill it up then get another one. It might take a bit, but this will begin helping you set your mood for your day as a happy one.

Then Exercise. You can move in some way. If you are in a wheelchair, you can move your arms. If you are bed ridden, move what you can move. Baby steps. Inch by inch is a cinch. You can do it. Blinking, breathing…. You can do something. Breathing exercises are both calming and can help the diaphragm. (Tummy muscles.)

There was a point in my life when they said my brain would not be full capacity again because of migraine. I proved them wrong. There was a point where the doctors doubted, I would not regain full mobility in my right shoulder due to a neck issue. I have full mobility. Why? I did not give up. I kept trying exercise routines that were gentle until I found a way to get there. That is a huge key. Don't give up. Even if you fall down, get up and get back on track. It took me 6 tries to quit smoking. Giving up cheese was an even harder struggle. Addiction is a powerful thing. I'm not saying it's easy. I'm saying keep trying until you get there. Don't give up. You can do it.

So, to conclude our addictions chapter, basically 4 key elements.

1. Start.
2. Gratitude.
3. Exercise.
4. Don't give up.

If you struggle with an anxiety, depression, mental, trauma, or PTSD issue, there are so many books on these subjects that will give you help. Please pick one and learn how to use some tools to get you through instead of alcohol or drugs. You can do this.

Before you say well you weren't really an addict, does it take an addict to see? Do you have to be lost to see the way out? I can assure you I have been down some dark roads that I thought I would never see the light again. My addiction to cigarettes was so powerful it took me 6 tries to quit. I am 10 years free of them. I am here to say there is light at the end of the tunnel. There is love after heartbreak.

I believe in you. God believes in you more. He believed in you so much that He sent is Son to save you. How amazing is that. He loved you that much.

FOUR

You Can Change Your Health

You really can change. First if you don't exercise start. Even if it is 5 minutes of whatever movement you can do, do it. Begin somewhere. Everyone starts somewhere. Exercise increases endorphins. Yeah, we all know it. We all don't want to. After you get started, you will begin to like it. Trust me. Try to increase it until you are doing 30 minutes 3 to 5 days a week.

If you have a medical issue, please check with your doctor, and find something safe for you to do. Your health is important to me, to God, and to your loved ones.

Second get a notebook. (No, I am not going to ask you to journal. You can if you want to.) Every morning, write down 3 things that you are grateful for. Every evening write down 3 things that you are grateful for. Gratitude journals changed my perspective in life. That and my learning about God has brought joy back to my life.

When I started this process, I was extremely depressed. Many of my entries were simplistic. I am grateful I made it through the day. I am grateful for food. Then gradually they became I am grateful for friends. I am grateful for my ability to move or see. These are examples of things you can write down.

Your possibilities are endless. (People, favorite places, books, love, etc.)

Third count how much alcohol or drugs you consume. Cut back an amount a week. It doesn't have to be drastic. Even if it is 1. Cut back. Promise yourself. That person in the mirror is counting on you. Exercise and 3 things that make you happy should take up some of the time you were doing your weapon of self-destruction. If it doesn't take enough time at first, call a friend before you are drunk/stoned. Just call or text someone. Try to be away from the drugs or alcohol so you can really communicate. You know which friend takes how much phone call/text time. Some people are 15-minute calls. Some people are 5. Some are an hour. Get a cheerleader. (Someone who is helping you get there.) Someone in your life cares and wants to help you let that habit go. Maybe that person could be your call. Example: Hi (Person's name) I'm calling because I need to talk for ½ an hour to keep from drinking 1 beer. I am cutting back by one per day. Do you have time to talk for ½ and hour? Talk about the weather, talk about baseball, talk about work, it really doesn't matter what you talk about really. You can do this. I believe in you. God himself is on your side.

Start working on those lies right now. You are enough. You were enough before you were born. Your very existence matters to someone. You don't have to do or be anything. They love you just like you are. God and I love you just the way you are, and we want you to know you can do this. The power has always been right there in you. Everyday just waiting to emerge. The darkest places have a light you can't believe waiting in them to show you the way. Yours is inside you. I know, it was inside me. There in the dark I found the brightest light waiting to release me into a life of joy that I had never known before. It's in you too. The power is right there inside you.

Fourth. Eat better. Get more vegetables in. Less potato chips and cookies. If you drink soda, please stop. Replace it with water. You can add a slice of fruit for flavor. Diet pop is even worse than sugary pop. Please stop. If you stop that alone, you will feel better. Try having a meal with a beverage that is not alcohol.

Also, guess what, cheese is addictive. If you eat a lot of cheese.... Cut back. I know. That's a toughie. I was at a 2 lb. brick a week. Yeah, you can laugh, but I love Tillamook cheddar cheese. Now if I buy one it spoils. I ended up getting migraines. So, I had to say no to cheese until I could balance it. I looked at the doctor like he shot my dog when he said no cheese. I still must watch myself or I will get carried away with it. It is better for me not to have it in the house.

Water, Water, Water. Water helps you feel full if you are trying to lose weight. Water helps clear toxins out of your body. Water helps your kidneys and can reduce lower back pain from kidney issues. Water prevents dehydration. Water helps reduce headaches. Water cleans and heals your liver. So yeah. Drink water. It has a lot of benefits. 64 ounces a day at least.

Nutritionists and programs. Yes, and a big fat no. Just like all things in life there are good and bad ones out there. My program lines up with my doctor recommended nutritionist.

(So yes. It is working to get my numbers down and improve my health). It did not happen too quickly. World class athletes use nutritionists. Most of them are excellent. They will hook you up with proper portions and a balance that will stop your cravings in no time.

Here is the buyer beware. All programs are there to make money. Some sell supplements. I am not knocking supplements. If you need some, take some. There are some supplements that you may need. BUT if they are recommending you take extra maybe you should think about it. I took extra of a fish oil supplement. I ended up with fatty liver disease. As soon as I stopped taking that supplement, it went away. My numbers returned to normal. So, beware. Do your homework on supplements. Get medical advice. Many supplements can build up in your body. Vitamin B for example can cause symptoms similar to neuropathy if you take to much and it builds up in your system.

I got another program that is nutrition based. <u>Vonda. Derkson@Beachbody.com</u> can do wonders for you. Vonda is an excellent coach. She is both highly motivational and understanding. This works for me because I am not 20 anymore. Age related injuries happen sometimes. I must navigate pain related issues, arthritis and be able to get exercise back on track. Having a coach helps.

One quick thing about Beach Body programs. All are nutrition and exercise based. There are a huge variety of exercises to choose from for all body types from yoga to extreme and military fitness programs. You can start slow and work into what you can do. I love the reasonable pricing. I truly love military and extreme workouts. As you put some mileage on your body and a few years under your belt things happen that sometimes don't allow you to do things that you want to with your body. (Depending on how hard the miles were.) I liked hard physical activity when I was young. I lifted too much. Tried to keep up with the men too much. (I was never enough for me. But that is another book.) If you do hard things to yourself long enough the damage you do will begin to cause you problems and you will have to adjust.

Starting slow is one thing I had to do as an adjustment. My doctors have told me many times you won't get that back. You won't get normal brain function back. (From migraine.) You won't get full movement out of your shoulder again. (Degenerative disk in my neck) I sometimes don't listen so well to these doctors. Here is how I start:

I ask what can I do? Don't ask yourself what you can't do. Ask what you can do? Start there. Take that no matter how small and work up from it.

My right arm could not reach high enough to brush my hair. I love to dance. I picked a low impact dance routine. I could not lift my right arm up all the way when I first started but I started and continued to do the routine 5 days a week and continued to try to raise the arm a little more each time. Sometimes it would sometimes it would not. I kept going and stretching like the physical therapist recommended. Was it easy? NO. I did not push to pain. I just tried and kept going. (Vonda was amazing and encouraging.) After 10 months I reached up one day, and my bicep touched my ear. Hallelujah. Yes. It just happened. I let go of any result. I had no expectation I would get that result. I just tried. So, let go of result and try. You have nothing to lose by seeing where you can go. You are looking to get somewhere just going on a journey with a small habit that is good for you. Don't even set a goal to get somewhere. Set a goal to be healthier. Just stay the course.

Pick something you like. If you don't like it, you're not going to do it. If there is nothing you like, reward yourself with something you like afterward. (Not ice cream. Ha ha.) Say you need exercise and decide to walk. After a certain number of miles buy an outfit, pair of pants, pair of shoes, it could be anything really, treat yourself to a day at the beach, river, park, or video store. I don't know what it is that makes you happy but some treat that isn't harmful to you.

Let's talk weight loss or gain. What is too quickly? This will vary from person to person. When you first start a program, you will lose more weight or gain more (depending on goal) because you changed your habits. After a time that will slow down and eventually it will stop. I am not at a point in my life to advise you on breaking through that yet. I have not yet broken through. A nutrition coach would be better suited for that. All I know is if you quit you go backwards and that isn't the direction, we are interested in.

Let's talk people. People are great for support. I have been in some support groups that would knock your socks off. They were super helpful. They drifted away. A long time ago my mother said to me "Nothing is forever." I took it to mean love doesn't exist do whatever you want and ran around making no sense to anyone. (That's another story.) Let me explain it another way. People are great for support, but we are all only borrowed. No one person can be your everything, every day, every second, …That is God. Don't try to make people be your God. It's unfair to them and you. Someday God needs all of us back. All of us here have missions that we need to accomplish, don't get in the way of someone's mission. Love every second that you have with your people. Don't forget to tell them what they mean to you. We never know how much time we will get. I hope that is what mom meant by nothing is forever. Love you Mom. Let people inspire you. Believe me they are trying. Let them support you but don't rely on them for your sole means of support. Some of it must come from inside yourself. Start telling yourself supportive things. God loves you, you can too.

Plateaus will come. My plateau hit right as covid hit. The opportunity to increase exercise was not there and my eating habits decreased at the same time. There are times when we fall. Guess what? Get up. Brush yourself off. Get back on track. Success doesn't me we didn't fail or fall off our horse. Success means we kept on trying.

That is exactly what I did. I got up. Said knock it off. Got a job closer to home.

Got back on track. Got rid of the job too far away for me to exercise. Stopped with the sugary beverages. I was only drinking them to stay awake for the 10 hours a day at the too far away job. Started exercising again. Got nutrition back on track. Drinking my water. Feeling better. Less than 3 weeks. So, if you fall down just get back up. I failed 5 times with cigarettes. I kept trying. Now I am 10 years smoke free. Each time I learned more about what worked and what didn't. Keep what works throw out what doesn't.

Don't be afraid to give yourself the leadership you need. You are worth keeping on track. Get in that mirror and encourage yourself. You are worth every second you spend helping you. That person in the mirror is counting on you and so are the people that love you.

You have some tools to get started. Here's where you need supportive friends. People who have been there. People who will encourage you no matter what.

Scripture to back you up? 2 Timothy 1:7 For God hath not given us a spirit of fear, but a spirit of power, and of love, and of a sound mind.

Are you reading this for a friend or loved one with an addiction? God Bless You if that is the case. I both feel and understand your pain. I have been there.

Alanon says all you can do is love them through it. You know that person better than I do. You know how to love them. Please do not enable them. That is not love.

I found that saying I love you and I need you to be present in our conversations helps. I don't want you to die helps. I am concerned about your health. These are things that show true caring.

Truthfully that person will only quit when they decide to. You can encourage them even if it is their 70th time that they have quit. Encourage them and believe in them. They need it.

I quit smoking. Second hardest thing I have done. (Chocolate was harder.) I tried 6 times to quit. My 3rd through 6th time people said yeah sure, you're going to quit. None of them believed. (It is heartbreaking.) To an alcoholic or drug addict, you might as well be saying it's ok, we know you can't do it. Don't discourage them. Negative thought patterns will never help anyone. Don't give them anymore than they already have working against them. Quitting a habit is hard.

When you expect someone to fail you encourage them to fail. Encourage them to succeed. Believe in them. As many times as it takes.

 FIVE

Depression and Anxiety

I mentioned before that I have had some dark days. I struggle still on occasion. I am grateful the darkness of depression is infrequent now. This chapter is the one that I know the most about. I struggled with depression for 26 years. I planned my death many times. I think too much. If I leave my mind idle it will chew on itself. I thought of it as depression, but I recently discovered that I may have been suffering from anxiety. I will discuss both.

I was on and off antidepressants. They would work awhile and stop working. I got so tired of the cycle. Most likely I did not express this correctly to my doctors and was misdiagnosed. The human system is complicated.

Many of my dark moments no one could reach me. I could be laughing with you and feel nothing inside but emptiness. Be in a crowd and feel completely alone. Be with my family or friends and feel completely alone. Most of the time I felt I didn't belong anywhere.

Love and light couldn't seem to breach my darkness. The gloom and despair were so heavy it was hard to breathe or take another step.

I felt so phony because I was going through the motions of my life doing my job perfectly and quietly so one noticed how I felt. Putting on my fake smile every day. Laughing and joking like nothing was wrong. It just made me feel worse. Outside I appeared so happy. Inside I just wanted to die.

One time I was going to kill myself by a river. It flooded. Something always got in my way. Something always kept me from being able to accomplish ending my life. Another time I took a bunch of sleeping pills but all it did was mess me up for a few days. I always felt no one cared and no one loved me.

I mentioned that I stopped doing drugs and alcohol and that had a positive effect on my depression. That was only the first step.

I read somewhere that gratitude journals helped, and exercise helped. I was always reading about how to fight this darkness. I decided to start keeping a gratitude journal. It wasn't far to work so I started walking to work as soon as I could walk a mile. (I started with a block). Gratitude journals are also listed in the anxiety books as a helpful tool.

My beginning entries were sad. I am grateful I made it through today. I am grateful I survived. It was hard for me to think happy things in that dark space, but I kept trying. After a time, the entries got better like I am grateful for sunshine and birds. I am grateful for friends and smiles. I am grateful for the ocean. I am grateful I can see and move. I am grateful to feel good. I am grateful to be able to move. I am grateful to have family.

My exercise increased to 5 miles in a few months, and I was feeling good. I was happy. I began to feel better about myself. I wasn't out of the dark yet, but things were so much better.

Then I started thinking about what I would like to do. I started pursuing hobbies that I liked doing. Life became an amazing journey.

I met people that liked doing what I like doing. It was fun. Life became fun. I was happy for the first time since childhood.

Here are a few other tips. Vitamins. Vitamin D is helpful if you don't get sunlight. Pacific Northwest area residents do not get enough sunshine so take vitamin D. Pay attention to the recommendation for dosage or ask your doctor if you need this.

November and December also bring bad foods. Sweets and carbs no one needs. Pies and cookies and parties oh my. All of that will throw you off balance in a heartbeat.

Here is one you may not have thought of medical and dental work. Any type of trauma to the body or anesthesia can throw your body off a little. Drink lots of water and remember you might be a little off. Get your work done though. Don't deny your health.

Now what about anxiety? Because I never experience a panic attack, I did not know I suffered from anxiety. I am certain after reading the book for a friend who would never read the book and learn it to help themselves that there are varying degrees of this.

Anxiety not only exists as full-blown panic attacks where people think they are having a heart attack. Some people will start thinking on a subject and overthink it. It could start with gas prices and end up with riots and not being able to get to your family. Or maybe a plane trip and it crashes and then what is your family going to do without you there. Or simply waking up afraid that your whole family is dead. Maybe it is milder like scenarios at work have you thinking that your work is inferior to everyone else and you're one step from a layoff, getting fired or no one likes you. Does your mind do this? That is anxiety my friend. I think all of us experience it to a certain degree. It's ok there are a lot of tools to deal with this.

First take a breath. What anxiety means is that you are a highly intelligent person, and your brain is looking for something to work on. Give it something.

Change the story. Words that we tell ourselves are very powerful. Make sure you are saying the right ones. If the story in your head has gone in a negative direction move it the opposite way. For example, I was reorganized once. Everyone got a new title except me. My mind started grinding on every mistake I made in a year. I grabbed a pen and paper wrote all that stuff down starting with everyone got a title except me. Then I started writing reasons it could be a good thing. Not everyone made the list. Maybe the people on the list might get hired and those not on the list are part time workers due to school. When you change the story, you aren't upset anymore. I was able to take that example to my friend with anxiety and show them an example of working through the problem in a positive way. I helped someone else with it. This is an imaginary example.

People with anxiety are extremely smart. Their minds are always working. You will hear them say I can't shut my mind off. I used breathing exercises and meditation in high school to help me sleep. This is one reason so many people self-medicate with drugs and alcohol. A much healthier way is meditation and exercise. Both will help your body relax more and help you sleep better. Melatonin does help. Try to stick with natural supplements. They are less harmful but check with your doctor if you are on medication. Some supplements can interact with medications.

If you need to stop the thought process all together because it has gone to such a bad space that you just need to stop it altogether. The 5 4 3 2 1 method is very helpful and calming. Think of 5 things you can see. Be sure to view them in detail. (I see my philodendron with green leaves and a touch of yellow and white). Think of 4 things you can touch. Describe that in detail. I feel the rough surface of an unfinished piece of wood that I'm working on. I feel the breeze on my face from a fan. Think of 3 things you can hear. I can hear the rain on the window. I can hear the tv in the other room. Think of 2 things you can smell. I can smell the dirt in the plant I just repotted. I can smell my coffee. Think of one thing you can taste. I can taste my coffee.

After this exercise you should experience a clear head. Sometimes you can just do some deep breathing and it will clear your head. I use this a lot. I breathe and repeat release to myself as I exhale. I let go of whatever thought or activity I was doing. Relax you body while doing this.

If you are in a loving relationship. You can have that person talk through some scenarios with you. Positive ones. None ending in death ok. Here is an example; I come home with anxiety about a work issue. I explain my boss wants me to take on this new project, I think he's setting me up to fail. OK. This is the partners turn. OK honey lets walk through a couple of things that could happen, so you are prepared. What's the worst that could happen? Let them explain their fear. Walk them through, how is that so bad or so different from now? Gently. Then talk the next worse. The next one down and the next. Eventually you will have de-escalated this fear to a calm state and prepared them for anything. Now the anxious person is ready for anything. Again, this is an imaginary scenario.

Let's walk through an example. Person 1 says: My boss asked me to take a test. I think they are setting me up to fail. They want to fire me.

Person 2 says: Oh, wow honey that must feel awful. Let's walk through what could happen. That way we have a plan. What's the worst that could happen?

Person 1 says: I fail the test. Person 2 says: Have they said they would fire you if you failed? Person 2 says: Well not really, in fact He told me he really needed me and would like to promote me.

Person 1 says: So, this test is part of a step that might get you promoted?

Person 2 says: Maybe I guess so.

Person 1 says: OK so if you do fail it where would they put you then.

Person 2 says: They have like 6 other jobs onsite or offsite that I can do.

Person 1 says: Your boss did say he needs you and he can use you in one of those right?

Person 2 should be feeling better now and not so anxious. Or Person 1 can continue with more scenarios. You get the idea of how this can work. Once again this is a made-up scenario for example.

If this is a first, try for you recognizing your partners anxiety it may take a little bit to adjust. Keep trying.

It may not be easy. It is worth it. You already have that pattern in your relationship. In my relationship, I have dismissed these feelings so many times that when I first tried this it was clunky and awkward. Keep trying. It will get better. If you have a loving relationship with someone you can talk. If you can talk some it will get better as you open those communication channels. Prayer and perseverance. Keeping a relationship is always about not giving up on each other.

The best thing that I found was finding out what God thinks about me. Finding out who I am in Christ brought a huge change to my life. First, I learned that when I was saved all debt was paid. Past, present, and future sins are wiped clean. This means that I am always clean and whole. I am always loved by God and Jesus and always in his favor. This was done because God loves me. 100 percent loves me no matter what. Even if I stumble, He will love me. This news brought such joy to my heart.

After I learned that great news, I learned about the tremendous resurrecting power of Jesus. When you are saved, That power lives in you via the holy ghost! That is tremendous news. You have all the power you need to break free from any destructive thought, addiction, anxiety. No bond can hold you. You can do all things through Christ who strengthens you. Philippians 4:13

SIX

··

Help Yourself Through and Talk

People that know me know I talk to myself. Only the words have changed. I was very mean when I was younger. I had a constant dialogue of you are not good enough. If this, is you, stop now? You hear yourself more than anyone else. Be kind.

God loves you. You can too.

I am serious. You need to start thinking of yourself the way he does. Let's talk about how.

Mind of Christ. 2 Timothy 1:7 For God hath not given us the spirit of fear: but of power, and of love, and of a sound mind. It took me a couple times to really hear this one. Are you listening now? Go back and read this paragraph a second time. Let it sink in.

Fear is brutal. It keeps us from doing things, going places, and speaking up when we should. Fear holds us to old patterns that don't serve us anymore. Fear keeps us down. Let fear go. Fear is not your friend.

I spent a lifetime not saying anything. Having all these thoughts, knowing the answers, and not speaking up. Not telling people how I truly felt and letting things eat away at me. Stop it. The world needs your voice. Studies have shown that if everyone collaborates on a project you get better results and reduce risk. The more diverse the better. Diversity and inclusion can improve all the results in a company. If you are thinking something different stop holding back. If it isn't recognized this time maybe next time. Sooner or later, you will hit on the next greatest idea. Your ideas have value. We are all different for a reason. The important thing is you will have said something.

Two things happen when you stifle your voice. You destroy your own integrity. Yes, you live a lie. You aren't being honest with yourself or others. People feel it. People will say about you, I always felt like they were holding something back. Like they weren't telling me everything. (They won't trust you because of it.) No matter how honest you are. The second thing that happens is your ideas stay silent. That great idea doesn't come out. Or you resent someone else for having your idea. Get those brilliant ideas out.

The best thing you can do with fear is face it. Look it right in the eye and run towards it. Pray to God and go for it. Failure is only a steppingstone.

So, the person you like doesn't share that affection. At least you know instead of wonder. Believe me you don't want to be with someone that doesn't love you.

So, you don't get the job. At least you know instead of wonder and maybe it will lead to a new idea or opportunity. Sometimes you have been blessed by this.

Try. Get up and get going. You are not a paperweight. Life is meant to be lived not sat through.

You owe it to your loved ones to tell them when something is bothering you. Is it easy? Probably not. If you're like me and you're always trying to pretend that didn't hurt so you can keep smiling and keep running on with your day, it is easy to let things slide awhile. Just recently I was struggling with this very thing. I was unhappy. Where is it that I got off track. What exactly is it I was unhappy about? See? Other people do it too. Get too busy to notice their feelings and soon we're off track. Seriously, most of the time I just want to work. I don't want to feel things. Haha.

Let's talk through it. First take an account of everything in your life that you are doing. Do those things make you happy? Is there anything that you could change about those things that could make you happy? For example, I increased my workload at work it was too slow. Don't be afraid to ask for more/less work. If you have too much, ask if someone could take 1 or 2 items to help you get it done so you can spend time with family. Get what you need.

Second are you feeding yourself the right "stuff?" Are you listening to things that make you happy or bring you down? Listen to uplifting things. When we fill our lives with drama on social media and TV all we have is tension. If we fill our lives with positive and encouraging messages, we build our life in a positive direction. If you want to change your life start here. Reduce your time on TV and Facebook and I promise you your life will become happier. Put more bible time in. Hope radio station is always uplifting, and Victory network is also uplifting. Always positive 24 hours a day. If you must be on social media. Try filling your feed with positive influence. Quotes, pictures of things you enjoy, anything you like. Block drama when you can.

There is a lot of material you can turn to lift you up. The bible is the first thing. If you pay attention to that book, it is full of stories of people who were not perfect that God loved anyway. Just like you and me. God loves all of us. He may not like some of the things we do just like we don't like some of the action's others do. But he loves us just the same.

There isn't much on TV. Maybe some exercise programs. A few nature programs that don't have the global warming agenda to depress you. (Not saying anything about that just saying it is not a positive message. They never offer a solution.) If you offer problems and no solutions, you are only depressing. There are billions of brilliant people working on solutions every day. Look for it.

Does your church send a message of hope or gloom? Do your friends share hope or gloom? How are you feeding yourself? You owe yourself the best. I'm not saying to order Tony Robbins, but I am saying there are a lot of positive people like Tony Robbins making a difference by changing those thought patterns and heading their lives in a different direction. Tony Robbins has been helping people for a long time. I love him. You can choose him if you like. He is awesome. My point is find one that fits you. Maybe you can motivate yourself.

You don't have to go back to school if you don't want to. You must get up and head in a direction of your dreams. No one will get them for you. You must do that. I know what you're thinking. I can't because... I have kids, my husband won't go for that, I don't have the energy...what is your excuse? You can have excuses, or you can have results. WHERE THERE IS A WILL THERE IS A WAY. YOU CAN DO THIS!

There are trade programs, colleges (yes if that is your goal don't let me stop you.) You cannot become a doctor or lawyer without college. If that is what makes your heart sing go, get it. Do not sell that short either.

You have the power right in yourself to do anything you want to do. Happiness is saying I think I would like to try that and going for it. There is no one stopping you.

I recently wasn't feeling like my work life was going well. I volunteered for more work. It got me more fulfilling work. I had taken a project management course and I ended up getting a project management opportunity on a volunteer council. This is great work experience. Go get your opportunities. You can do it. I work for a company that listens. My supervisors listened and reorganized putting me in a position to receive more work. Get what you want.

There are classes you can do at lunch. Take time in the morning. Get up just a little earlier one day a week. There are all sorts of classes that are less expensive too. You don't have to break the bank to do it. Shop around. Look online.

Make sure you get what you need. Ask coworkers, friends, or family about classes that interest you. (Beware though this can bring some negativity and you need to not listen to that part.) Change makes friends think you are leaving them behind. It can create jealousy. Bless their hearts. They mean well.

Well-meaning family and friends can sometimes try to "Help" but can be so discouraging. These are not the people you will be listening to. You are going to listen to the people that believe in you.

Sometimes people will question what you are doing. Maybe even tell you it will get you nowhere. It isn't up to them where you are going. It is up to you.

My dream was to be an electrician. I pursued it with all my heart. Years of poor nutrition and poor nutritional understanding caught up with my body. Also, a lack of respect for my own boundaries. I lifted more than I should trying to prove to myself I was better than others.

You can do anything. You have nothing to prove. Set some goals. Start. If you need to adjust your goals, Look at them again in a month, or three months. Life is about starting, seeing what is working, changing, and adjusting to make it work. The most important thing is don't give up.

Here is what I want you to do. Start. Look up the class. Take 1 class. Take a free class at lunch. Find a time. There is a place you can put the time to learn something new toward your goal. Find out what you need to accomplish your task. Find out who does it well. Find out how they got there. You got this. Now it can be any class. Painting, writing, exercise, bookkeeping, excel, word, or even an online tutorial. Just try something. You've heard of the 20-minute concept? Give 20 minutes a day to some goal. You will achieve it I guarantee it. Or at least move in a direction that provides you with another fun opportunity. Look how things turned out for me. I am excited to go to work every day. I wrote this book in 20 minutes on 1 day a week.

Next step. After you finish that class. Look at yourself in the mirror. Do you feel different? Yes, keep going. No, keep going. Why? All things take time. When I started as a Technical Writer I felt like a complete failure. I even had a meltdown one day. I cried.

I was learning a new career in my mid 50's and I was not remembering things as easy as I used to. I did not want to leave my former occupation but could not do it physically. I'm trying as hard as I can to learn and every document I produce is getting rejected. I'm missing stupid things that I didn't even see. I'm doubting myself more than I ever have. So, I had to go ahead and cry. Let it out. Take a step back. Talk to a friend. Regroup. Think about quitting but don't do it. Then take what I have and give it a look. Figure out what is working and what is not working. Pitch what isn't. Keep what is. Move forward. Have a chat with my boss intelligently about things. They respect it if you don't have a meltdown.

After my cry, I picked myself up and kept going. Most important step? Keep going. If you give up, you lose and so does everyone else. No one will ever know how great you could have been if you quit. Keep going. (Also, I have a great memory. Things take time when you bite off a whole new career.)

I believe in you and so does God. Please start believing in yourself. God bet on you so much that He sent His son to die for you so that you could be saved. How incredible is that!? God believes in you, so can you. He knows everything about you right down to how you were created. He loves you so much that He gave His son not to lose you. Jesus gave everything so that you could experience that love.

OK? There is nothing left but to get started. Go get those dreams. Don't give up.

God and I are rooting for you. (I bet you have more people in your corner than that.)

The Power is in You.

SEVEN

Life Changing Power In You

When I was 5 years old at a little church in Brownsville, Oregon in the month of June 1969, I was born again. My Christian walk began. It was not always perfect as you can tell by the things I have mentioned earlier in this book.

I ran from the truth. I ran from God. Until that day in the darkness. Even though I ran every step of my life I can still see his hand protecting me. Many of the things I did could have ended very differently. Many things could have gone very badly but they never did. I do believe He was always there in the background waiting for me to see my foolishness. Waiting for the prodigals return. His love really is that deep for us.

If you are not saved, you can be. All you need to do is say: Dear Lord Jesus, I know that I am a sinner. I believe you lived and died. I believe you rose again so that I could be born again in the spirit. Right now, I turn from my sins and open the door of my heart and life to you. I receive you as my Savior, come into my life and save me. Amen

This will begin your walk with Jesus. The holy spirit will come into your life and do the rest. Any life changes you need will happen through learning about God.

Let's talk about that first verse 1 John 5:4 again. It is the power that is given to you when you get saved. That is why it is important to get saved. Someone once asked me "Why is that important as long as I believe?" The help of God through Jesus Christ comes from it that's why. I don't know about you, but I don't want to struggle through everything in my life. I want the comfort of knowing it's handled. I want the comfort of knowing that just doing my best, praying for guidance and God will handle the rest is enough. I know me. I know I will mess it up. I assure you; I made a complete mess of my life before I came to God. I said, "I can't do it anymore. If you can do something with my life it is yours." That day changed everything for me. I began to see miracles all the time. My pay increased twice in a month. My $25,000 debt dropped to $5000 in that same month. That was only the beginning.

I began to care about myself. I began to see that I am worth loving. God loves you, why don't you. If the creator thinks so much that he doesn't want you to be lost, well maybe that should make you think you are something special too.

It made me begin to associate with more challenging people and people that like me for who I am, not what I can give them. I began to grow in ways that helped me get to what he wants me to do. I began to be able to see projects with what outcome could be. (See the beauty.)

I began to look at life differently. I looked at myself differently. I looked at others differently. I learned the meaning of love. I learned that love had power.

I began to get focused and organized. Finding new ways to organize my time to get my book writing time in. I began to encourage myself with scripture, books, positive people, and time in the mirror. I set further goals and grew my accomplishments. I gave myself raises. I had setbacks and gave myself raises again. Doing this will help you feel better.

Life began to grow and change in my friendships and relationships. I made time for friends and family. (I always tried but nothing but worked before.) This gave me more encouragement. I found out my family always believed in me. Then I found out God loves me.

What does this mean for you? This means you can too. I want you to get up and discover you. I want you to get in touch with that person deep inside. Really know who you are. Be that person every day. That person is happy and ready to immerge. That person is confident. That person is strong.

Earlier I talked about feeding your spirit. Feeding your spirit is very important to your wellbeing. All humans have a spiritual nature. Science backs this up. Prayer/meditation is good for you. It helps your body. Prayer is a form of meditation. It doesn't take a long time, so I encourage you to start your day with that and exercise. Get to know how much God loves you and what He says about you.

Jesus is the most powerful tool you can have against depression, anxiety, or addiction. (Health issues, or anything else that could possibly ail you.) When you invite Jesus into your life something amazing happens. I am certain that you have heard that he comes into your life and cleanses your spirit. (Makes you whiter than snow). Do you know what that means?

I love the number 3. The Holy Trinity. Father, Son and Holy Ghost. We are made in His image. We have a body, soul and spirit. (Hmm another 3)

The body is physical. Living breathing. Have to feed it the right foods and exercise so it will perform. We know how those functions. See chapter 4.

Your soul is your brain/mind. You have to feed it the right information. Feed it news and negativity and it will be sad/scared/afraid. Feed it the bible and it will get empowered. If you focus on scripture and teach your brain what is lovely and true, I can promise you it will make a huge difference in your life.

I have many resources for this. HOPE107.9 is an absolutely fabulous positive uplifting radio station. Victory network is great if you like television. 24 hours a day you can have some positive going in. The bible, you can choose a version.

Feeding your mind, the right thing is critical. Your thoughts direct your steps. If I start thinking about food. What happens? I start to feel like getting a snack or I get hungry. If I start thinking about the beach what happens. I start wanting to go to the beach. You get the picture. Where your mind goes the body follows.

Spirit. Before we are born again, we have a carnal spirit. It is dead to God due to sin. When we ask Jesus to come into our hearts Jesus replaces that dead spirit with his spirit. (Holy ghost filled spirit). Inside we are pure. Our spirit is whole and acceptable to God. It is the only way we can be perfect and acceptable to God.

That spirit inside of you can do anything. You get in touch with that spirit by renewing your mind with scripture and releasing your faith.

It's ok if you need to read that again. This is a real game changer. You have all that power of Jesus right there inside you. You have the power to walk away from cigarettes, drugs, and alcohol for good.

You have the power to reclaim your health. You have the power to be happy. You can change your thoughts forever.

I am not staying dump all your medication. (Many medications have ways of reducing before stopping. Work with your doctor please.) I tried this once. You can seriously cause yourself harm coming off medication improperly.

I am saying change is possible. I am saying you have the power to change your life right inside you. It was given to you on the cross.

Love yourself every day because God does.

EIGHT

Conclusion

It really doesn't matter who you are, you are worthy of God's love, and you are here to do something. You have the power inside you to change yourself, influence others, or maybe the world. That is" The Power in You.". Everyone has it.

It doesn't matter where you are starting from. God loves you and will help you every step of the way. If you let Him guide you, you can go anywhere. All doors will be open in His perfect timing.

Let go of those things that don't serve you. Let go of your addictions. Let go of those idols that really aren't there for you. Let go of those destructive behaviors. Have you thought about your addiction or destructive behavior being an idol? It is. It's something you are trying to fill God's place with. That spot that seems eternally unfulfilled. You're trying to fill it with the wrong thing.

Let go of the things that are destroying your health. Get your exercise in. Get proper nutrition. It's too expensive? Do you have a small space? Can you raise a couple tomato plants? How about something else? Visit a fruit stand? Befriend a farmer. Learn about different vegetables in the store. Try different meats. Experiment with recipes. Have fun with this with a friend. Vegetables in season are the least expensive.

I learn more each day. I get in my bible and read every day. Each day holds something new. Each lesson I learn from a televangelist, or a church holds something great for me. Let God direct your life. All scripture is good for healing.

When he is in charge you will really learn. You will really grow. People will say things to you that you need to hear at the right moment. The power in you is God shining through. It was given to you at rebirth, with your first breath, and nothing can take it away from you. All you must do to activate it, is get up and try every day.

Fight depression with gratitude lists. Looking at the world differently is key to beating this. Get a positive peer group. Check in on and complement each other.

Talk to yourself positively. Always give yourself a hand up not a push down. Be your own positive peer group. Cheer lead yourself. Read yourself scripture that tells you positive messages.

Your have had the power in you all along you just didn't know how to use it. He walks with us every day. We have that voice inside to guide us. He is with us. I love you, God does to, and you can too. Allow your power to flow every day. Get in Gods word and back up your truth with his word.

His guidance will be found in scripture. That is how you will know it is true guidance from God.

Find a good program to learn about how much God loves you. Find out what God thinks about you. You will never look back. I can promise you that you will experience joy from that. Knowing God loves you personally is a powerful experience. Knowing he wants to see you succeed. Knowing he wants to see you happy. It is life changing.

I will close with a little prayer for you.

May our Father bless you as He has blessed me with joy in your heart and freedom from the bondage of addiction, depression and anxiety. May He help you be a blessing to those you seek to help.

Amen

Printed in the United States
by Baker & Taylor Publisher Services